LEARN
ICT AND SMART M
CONCEPT TRADING

JASPER FROST

What is an Orderblock

Order blocks are the pieces of institutional capital that enter the market algorithmically at key levels. Instead of entering hundreds of millions of dollars all at once, institutional orders are split up into several entries. This causes tight consolidations that we see right before the market moves impulsively. This method leaves a map with an institutional trace that can be seen and used.

The most important thing to understand about these institutional orders is that there is no protected stop loss. This is the reason (buying and selling at the same time): companies hedge their stocks. You might wonder why they would do that instead of just using a stop loss. The simple answer is for institutions to move the market without losing money.

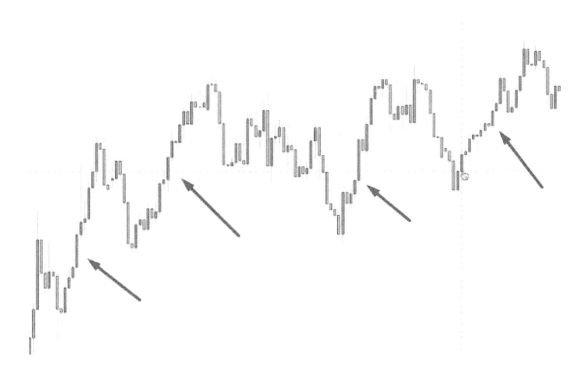

These big changes are the fault of institutions. All of these things are not done by retail sellers, and we don't make such big decisions.

What does that mean, then? How does that help us, then?

So, in effect, what we are doing with the plan is sharing the formal institutions' digital fingerprints.

How do you interpret that?

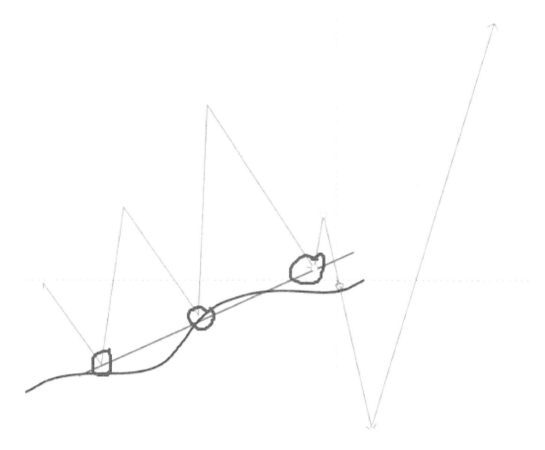

We are therefore in motion and enjoying a pleasant rise. We also have an excellent EMA and trendline. Has there ever been a situation when a trendline has one, two, and three touches, and we decide to trade on the third touch? In such case, what comes next? Occasionally, there can be a slight response and a drop in price.

What follows then?

The price decides to move in the direction we had planned to trade. We're all probably thinking, "Oh, that was just a stop hunt," at this point, and the truth is, it was. They are real.

How does that help us, and what does it mean?

Therefore, to use a normal retail approach, we need to understand what is happening in this case.

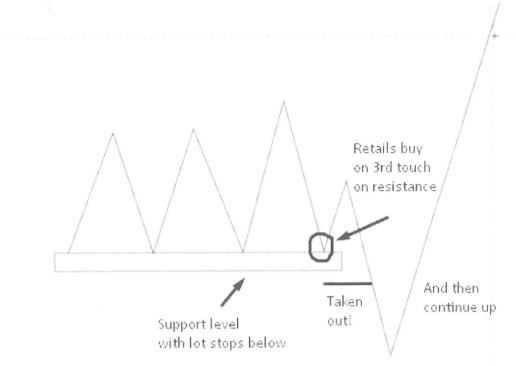

Retails buy
on 3rd touch
on resistance

Support level
with lot stops below

Taken
out!

And then
continue up

Have you ever wanted to enter a trade at a strong support level but were forced to wait for further movement, which is OK, before the price moved on and you were taken out? We have this strong support because many traders use resistance and support. You're probably thinking, "We just got taken out; my stops were hit, but I was right about the direction."

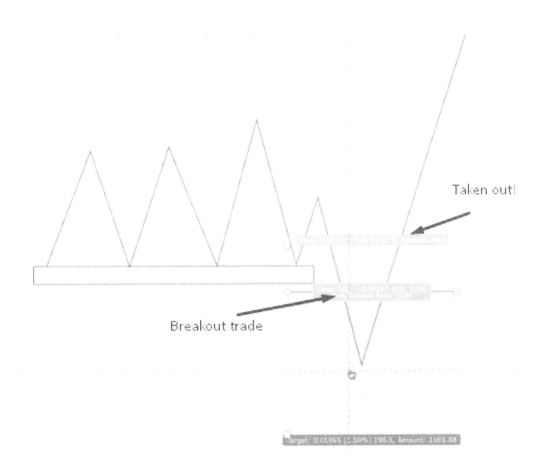

Taken out!

Breakout trade

Alright, well done, but the deal was still unsuccessful. Alternatively, have any of us ever been breakout traders who anticipated price action and entered a trade at the breakout? If such was the case, we saw the breakout and concluded, "Yeah, I know I got it right," but in the end, we failed. We are completely misguided in that interaction.

Why is that allowed to happen?

We must ask ourselves, "Why does that keep happening?" Although this method is predicated on probability, it ignores the real dynamics at play in the market and the players driving prices lower before they rise to our advantage.

We are aware that talent comes at a cost.

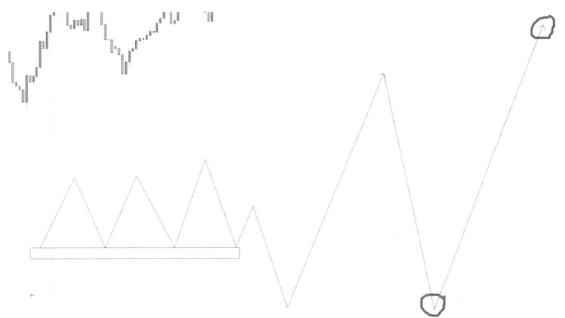

Why does the price go in this manner, reverse course, and then move forward once more? At this point, we're undoubtedly asking ourselves, "Why does it do that? " So let's take this approach to it. We are aware of resistance and support, as well as institutions.

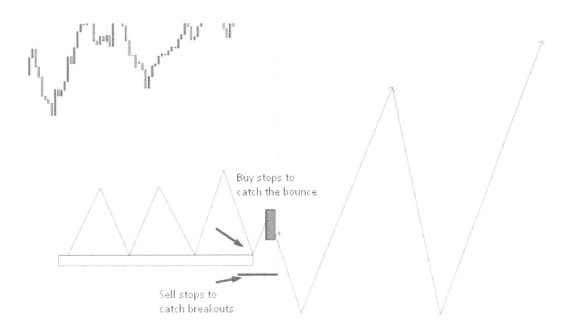

Buy stops to catch the bounce

Sell stops to catch breakouts

Consequently, we may deduce that orders are being placed at this time; sell stop orders are being placed to capture the breakout, and buy limit orders are being placed to capture the rebound.
But someone has to lose and someone has to win for the market to work. Consequently, you have to lose for me to win, and I have to lose for you to win. This is the terrible reality of how the markets function. Institutions are well aware of this widespread support and pushback.

Due to their dependence on probabilities rather than an understanding of real market activity, the classic trendline and fib strategies have been known to occasionally work and occasionally fail.

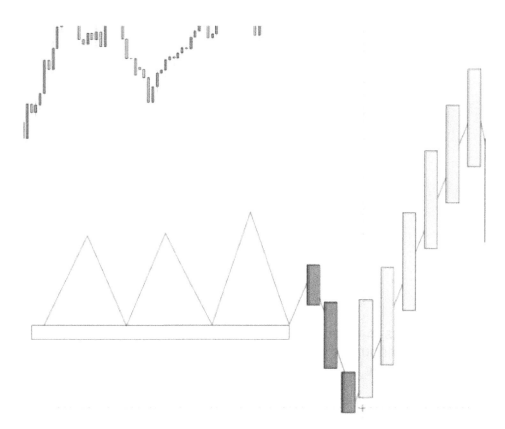

The price is being pushed lower, then increases momentarily before exploding higher again. In order to drive everyone to quit, the institutions are purposely driving the price lower before the rally, which sets off stop losses and sell orders for breakout traders.

The moment has arrived to take liquidity from breakout traders because, once they have enough liquidity, the price will rise.

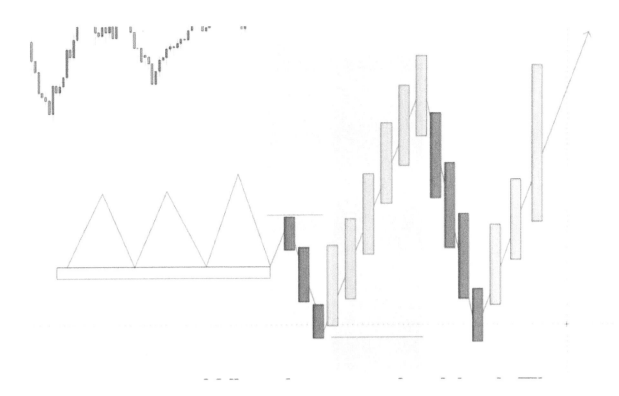

They had, however, always desired to embark on a long journey. They are going long from this position as a consequence, which is acceptable, but when we look at it from this perspective, we can see that they have to lower the price to get there, which calls for the creation of a sell position. However, they do not use stop losses. They gave up this position in order to drive the price up to where they could seize liquidity and make this move, but once the price reaches that point, they are left in a situation of drawdown because there is none. They are still losing money on the first transaction even if they are in a winning deal that is rising.

To finish the sell position and proceed upward, they must thus lower their orders and losses. This is what transpires because they don't want a loss...

So this comes into question, what is an order block?

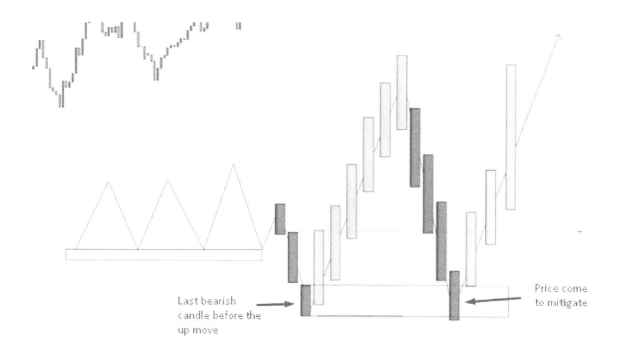

Last bearish candle before the up move

Price come to mitigate

The order block is essentially where the institutions put their last orders before to the move. Looking at it this way, then, where is that place? It is obvious that the author didn't want to draw that there because it is the final negative candle before the bullish surge. What is meant by that? It implies that before proceeding as they usually wish to, they must come and lessen their loss by shutting it at either a break-even point or a slight loss. Since it was the last location the institution sold before the price was increased, this is the order block.

Yes, it's true that they've always wanted to be bullish, but this transaction has to be closed since it keeps happening.

What does that mean, then? In what way does that help us?

Since we are aware that this mitigation is required and that the price will eventually rise again, we will attempt to enter at this point. Essentially, we want to make a trade to follow the trend from there.

Think of it this way: We are simply tracing the footprints left behind when we look for the final instructions that institutions have issued against the original action or the move they meant to make.

If they choose to go bullish, we will thus be watching for the last negative candle preceding the bullish move, which went against structure. That's the next important point.

Therefore, it needs to defy the structure in order to be considered an order block. We call this a break of structure, or BOS. Consequently, we can see that the order block has upset this arrangement. We are convinced that retail traders won't take any action that might jeopardize the structure as a result.

As everyone knows, this is the final negative candle preceding a bullish move and, conversely, this is the last bullish candle preceding a bearish move.

When a price breaks a structure and then, for example, keeps moving in the direction of the overall trend, we know that it is suspicious. Since the price initially created a low and a lower high (LH), broke to produce a new low, and then broke structure, we may conclude that the price broke the low that was being constructed.

How come it behaved that way? As everyone is aware, the general tendency is positive. Since this OB created the BOS, some SMC traders would issue a sell order from this position, even if it has taken liquidity from the prior low.

Daily chart

However, the institutions have advocated for this reform. Large impulses indicate that institutions were clearly engaged at the time, but the price suddenly broke the structure, and if we look at it daily, we can see that it breaks the structure every day. The strong desire has not yet materialized as retail traders are not yet making those deals.

Knowing what the OB is now allows us to observe that it is the last bearish candle before the bullish rise.

The answer to the issue of whether this is an OB or not is yes, as it is the last bearish candle before the bullish advance. But we are unable to pose the same query regarding whether or not that qualifies as an OB. But when we talk about refining, it will become more evident why these are both as appropriate in terms of being an OB.

The structure has been disrupted by a bullish move, just as what is happening presently. Before the bullish advance, where was the last bearish candle? Is this person that we have an OB? No, since there were no BOS.

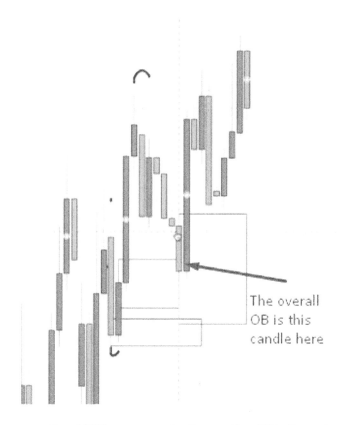

The overall OB is this candle here

This candle here on the HTF represents the entire OB, therefore this is where it makes sense. But it didn't lead to any structural collapses.

Can be this two candles to form OB, but this above is our OB now

Seen from another perspective, it looks like the OB is located exactly there. It's one of these two, however prior to the transfer, this was our OB in our situation.

We need to define an OB before we can move on. Stated differently, OB serves as the last site of institutional activity prior to migration.

In the event of a bullish advance, their OB is the last negative candle before the bullish rise. The OB for a bearish move that is set to decrease is the final bullish candle before a negative move.

They have to mitigate those transactions when price is returning to the OB at the last spot where they may have put sell orders, and that is where we will try to join the picture.

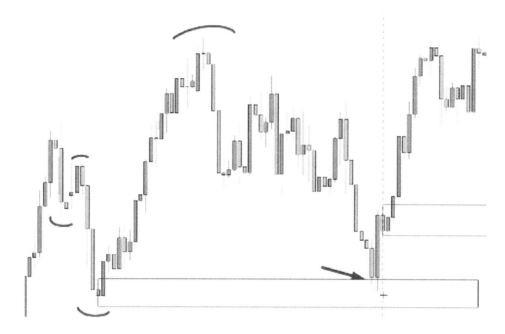

When this mitigating play is occurring, that is when we will try to join the trades. In essence, we are exchanging that footprint.

How to Refine Order Blocks

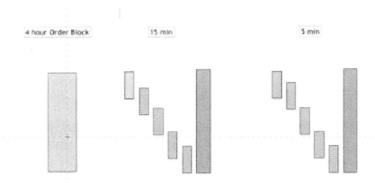

Assume for the moment that the 4H order block is the one we find. Now that we know, there are several little candles in this order block.

What do I mean by that, too?

We are aware that there will be several more candles before the price rises once more, say on the 15m. Then inside that, we have this repeating itself with extra candles, for example, at the 5m interval.

What do I want to convey with this?

For example, if we look at an order block for a bullish move, we will thus be looking for the last bearish candle before the bullish move happens. My blue candles are the bullish ones and my gray candles are the bearish ones in this situation.
As a result, we are aware that this 4H order block contains 15m and 5m candles. Now, if we are going to think about where they last sold, we are going to look at this candle (4H) and see where the sell orders have been put the most recently.

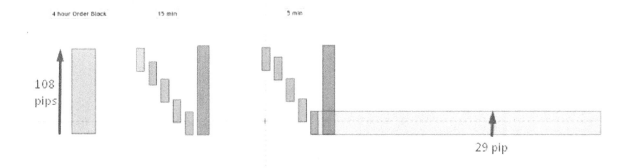

The last location orders have been placed is this candle, then. My order block is a polished 4H candle as a consequence. This 4H candle has now been cut to a 29 pip order block from its initial 108 pip order block.

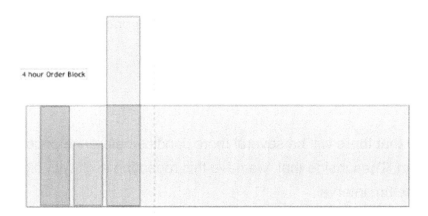

There's another method I could use to do this. Let's take an example where I have a 4H candle like this one, and then I have another bullish candle and yet another bullish candle. This is all happening at my OB right now. It is my knowledge that this is the OB candle. This candle is therefore 4H OB.

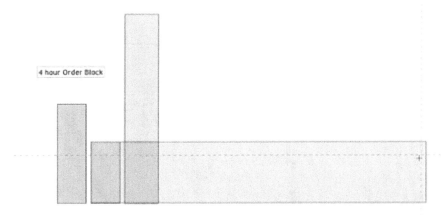

I can mark this out without the need for an LTF now that I know the OB's range, which is this. I may tweak it to add the wicks if the subsequent candle falls into the OB's range.

I may thus tweak the OB rather than lowering it to an LTF.

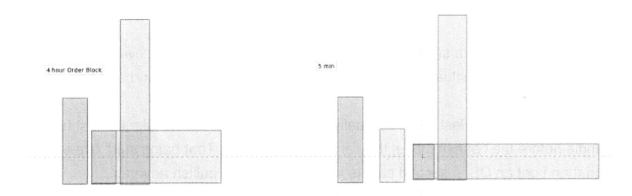

If I were in these conditions (4H), in these conditions (5m), or even in these conditions if I had another candle, bullish or bearish, the same thing would occur. Until it breaks the range, this gray candle—which we identify as the OB—keeps moving to the right. This candle is the last one to appear before the impulse expresses itself; it symbolizes the impulse and is still within the OB range.

To clarify, even though I have refined the 4H block to this one (5m), I still have this refined 4H OB and this candle inside this range. I have enhanced it without taking into account the different timings because this OB will be sitting on the 1 meter...

This is an instance of a situation that occasionally occurs. However, every now and again I find myself in situations such to this, where I get the desire and an OB is seated close by.

I have one where the last candle is really bullish before the move. Like the last bullish candle before the bearish move, they are simple candles. That being said, every now and then I get an OB, a second candle in between, and a bullish advance.

For example, if it falls within this range of the OB, I may just narrow it down to the next candle.

That being said, in this instance, I have a BOS, which indicates that this is the OB.

This candle is going to be the one to follow the instinct. In order to refine it to the one that is currently my OB, I don't need to decrease it to an LTF.

Right now, there is a bullish urge, and I will look for the perfect OB. The greatest OB will essentially be the most extreme one because it was the last site of the institution to be sold. Given that this is my OB, I would want to know where the institutions' most recent sale occurred prior to the price increase.

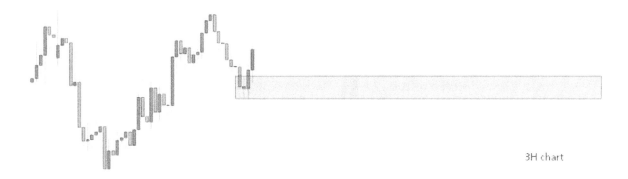

3H chart

I am therefore limited to visiting my OB and adhering to the schedule. When I go to 3H, it's still there.

2H chart

Look we can refine down to this one now.

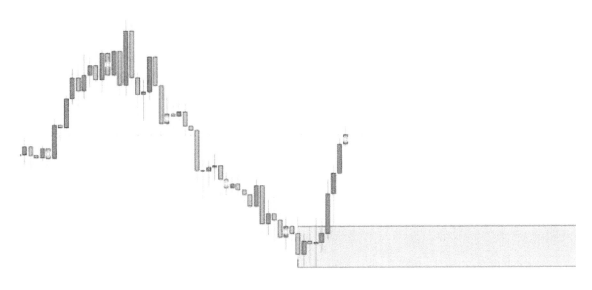

45m chart

If I want to, I can go to 45 meters, and nothing will change.

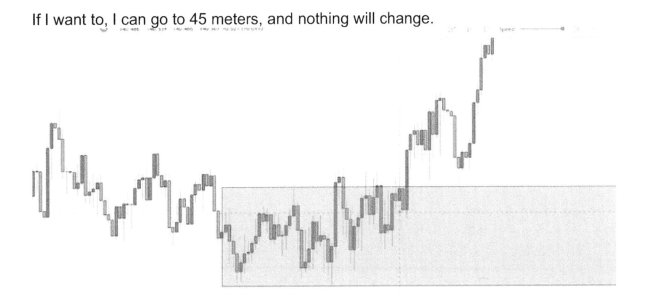

I will thus continue reducing the periods till I locate a distinct OB within this range. Once more, I wish to search for the farthest spot.

On the 4M chart, nothing makes sense to me.

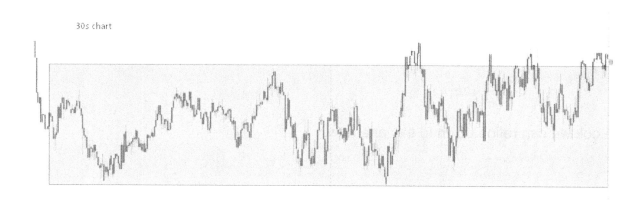

30s chart

Let's move on to the 1930s. What can I see? What will I have, then, if I zoom down within this?

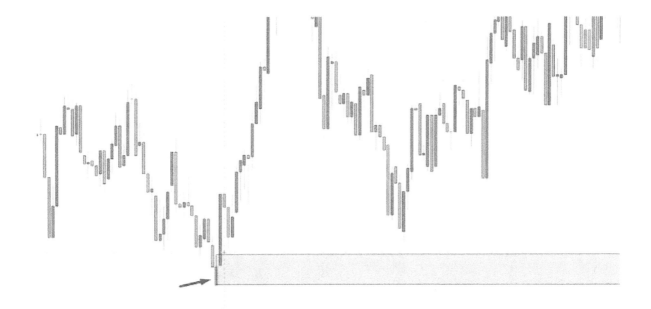

I have a small OB that is beneath the HTF OB that has not been mitigated. Institutions did not sell in this OB prior to prices rising further and not decreasing.

Why did I search for extremes yet not enjoy them?

Not this OB's because all are mitigated

Look for last place

is because everything is downplayed and nothing is made obvious. I have to find an OB that is mitigated. Thus, in order to reduce their OB, I want to think about where institutions should go last.

30s chart

← too close but not mitigated

Despite approaching, this 30-year-old OB in this role has not yet been mitigated since she has not yet reached her tapping out point.

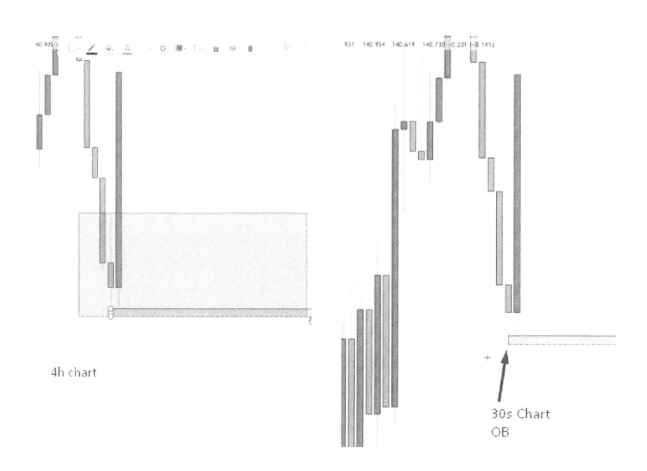

4h chart

30s Chart
OB

If I go back to the 4H, I can see that I refined the 4H OB all the way down to this. So, I'm expecting a response from this before prices increase.

4h chart

Price reacted precisely
and mitigated 30s OB

30s OB

Let's see what happens if I go back to where I was. The building was broken, and I'm looking for the OB right now. What is the purpose of the price? It came back, answered the 30s OB exactly, and continued. Examine how the price altered once the OB was reduced.

That's why it was so quickly denied out there: they can happily continue forward with their plan now that they have successfully lowered the OB.

That concludes the refining procedure. Therefore, all I need to do is reduce the timetables in order to locate an OB that I'm OK with when I narrow OB.

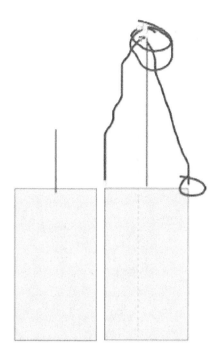

All of the OB is either inside the wicks or in this manner. Let's say this is a wick candle, and I have more candles like this one from time to time, and sometimes I make candles with huge wicks and sometimes I make candles with little wicks.

Right here, I can see what I desire.

Since the sellers are in control, the wick suggests that although the buyers are also raising the price, they finally become weary and that is why no one is there.

Why is that relevant?

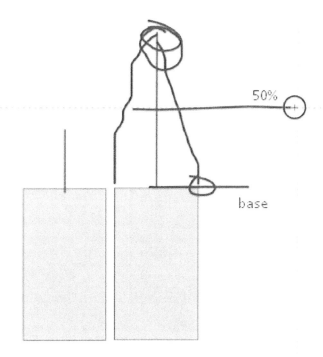

It suggests that this wick is where the sellers' pressure to sell is confined. The most crucial thing I want you to remember about this is that an OB occupies 50% of the base of this candle.

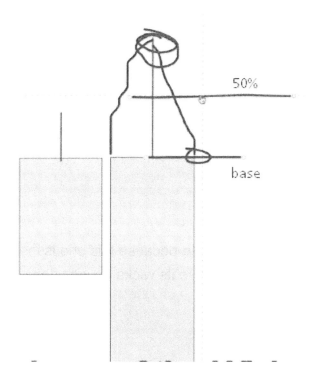

For the sake of illustration, let's say that is my OB and that is what I do next when I get impetuous. If the wick on my OB candle is higher than the one on the right, I could exchange.

I have my POI and am the 50% or the base of the wick. How I want to approach it is totally up to me.

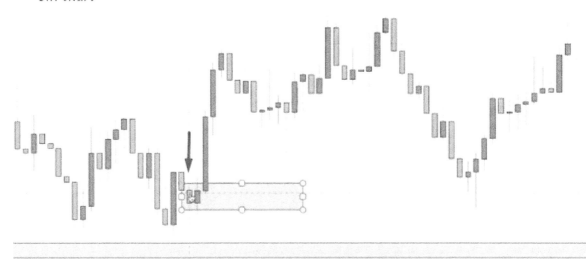

When I see it from this angle on the 5m, what can I see? As I have an on-the-spot broken BOS here, I can see the OB sitting here right away.

I may now move on to the next candle because this one is inside the range and hasn't gone outside the OB's range (because its wicks haven't done so, it isn't a candle body, and it hasn't).

This wick surpassing previous one

It has a new wick that works better than the old one..

Why does that matter?

Because the buyers own this candle, I can actually tailor my OB to that wick.

What is the reaction of the price?

It reacts because of that wick.
Before I can supply confidence that it is reacting to the wick and before I can get confidence that it is responding to OB, I need to have some experience. That's really where it comes from, because when I get a new wick, it goes down and takes the liquid out of the previous one.

The customers hold the power.

So what does that actually mean?

This is where the institutions are sold off last since that's where the purchasing desire started. That's why the vendors here are exhausted. Consequently, they have

This whole transaction originated here, with sales taking place all along this wick before to the substantial acquisition.

This is the last sell position, in theory.

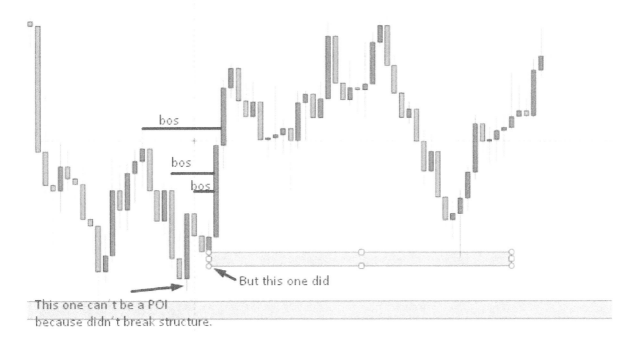

bos

bos

bos

But this one did

This one can't be a POI
because didn't break structure.

Because it didn't break the framework, it didn't do anything notable for us to signal that there is an OB sitting within it, but this one did. This one then produced a powerful move that brought down three buildings.
As a result, it has to be reduced, and that is what was done. I may have made a transaction based on it.

Is going just as it would, say, with the daily. Looking at it this way, where did the BOS happen?

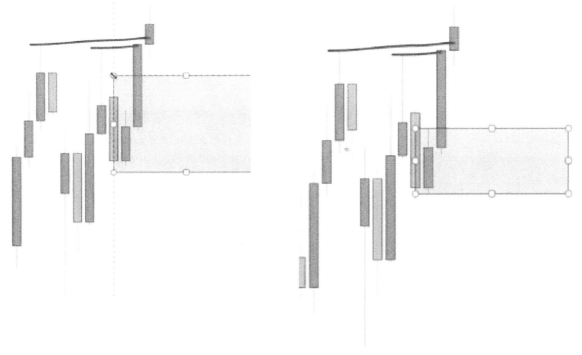

Thus, I've violated both of these structures. Where is the OB? This candle may be further narrowed down to the OB by lowering the timeframes, and then still further.

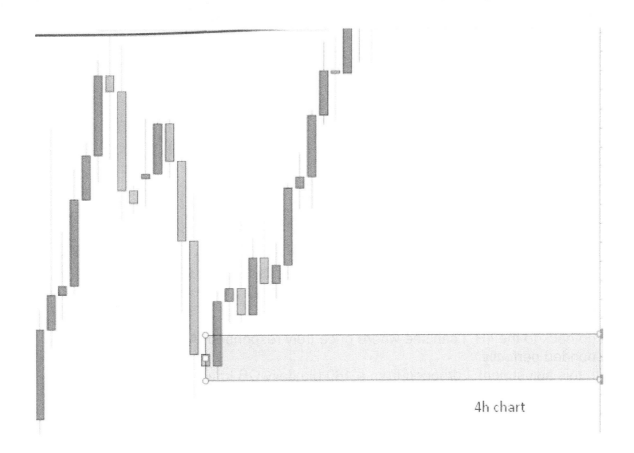

4h chart

Thus, I can narrow it down to this one and then continue to decrease the period and refine it even further until I locate a distinct candle that is an OB.

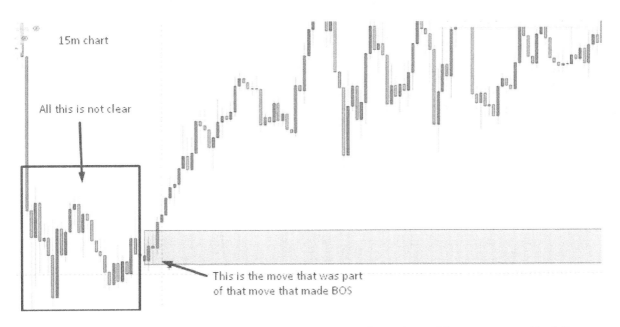

15m chart

All this is not clear

This is the move that was part of that move that made BOS

As best as I can tell, this is the one that remains unabated, and it was a result of the same activity that also demolished the structure. Nothing is very clear, even after only fifteen minutes.

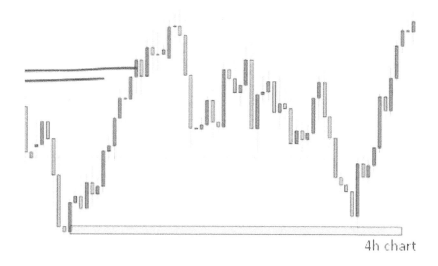

4h chart

If I go back to the 4H, I can see where price truly responded. As a result, the OB responded perfectly.

With this adjustment, I dropped from a 180 pip daily OB to a 9.8 pip 15 minute OB.

Imbalance

As far as I know, there has to be a 50/50 balance between buying and selling for the market to operate.

Why is that important?

It's because I frequently find myself in circumstances where, for example, I have powerful impulses. There is only buying. The markets don't work like that.

So what that mean?

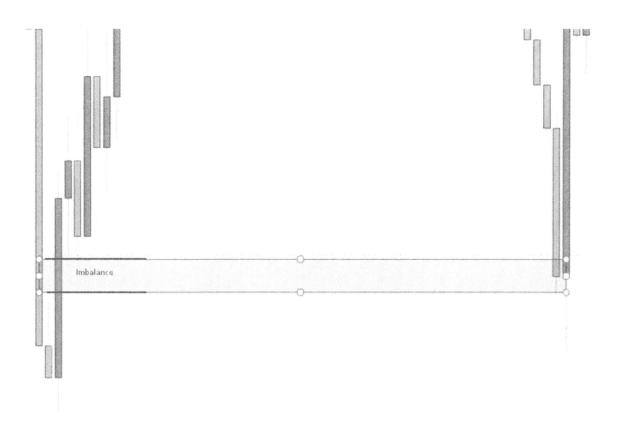

Price needs to show up and counterbalance this. We call this imbalance or inefficiencies. It's essentially the gap in the market. I can see that when I receive an OB or find one, there will probably be a gap, which serves as an example of the imbalance. Since there has only been purchasing, there is now an imbalance. I noted this box because, despite the bearish candle's wick, it is evident that sellers were active throughout that period.

Because sellers and buyers were driving the price back up at this point, buyers were participating in the wick. There is an imbalance because there is only one blue candle and all of the customers in this.

This means that even though I won't be trading directly off of it, it provides me with more proof that institutions were engaged in this OB. In other words, it basically implies that institutions were the ones who made this move and that regular traders are being negatively impacted by the imbalance.

Not lead to such an imbalance.

It is still unbalance even if it is only one pip. Pricing must thus be used to offset this imbalance, which gives me even another incentive to select this OB.

I want to look for a clear OB with a clear imbalance sitting over it anytime I hear someone say they want to find a clear OB.

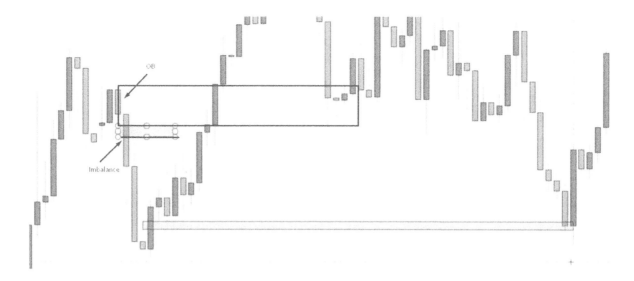

This also holds true for a bearish trend, which is why, using this OB as an example, I can see that it refines to the following candle. I act that way mostly because, when I look at it from the standpoint of where the wick is, the imbalance is between that wick and this wick right here. This is the candle that is before the impulse and the candle that has the imbalance.

Price must eventually show up to balance that out. Though it need not occur immediately, it must ultimately.

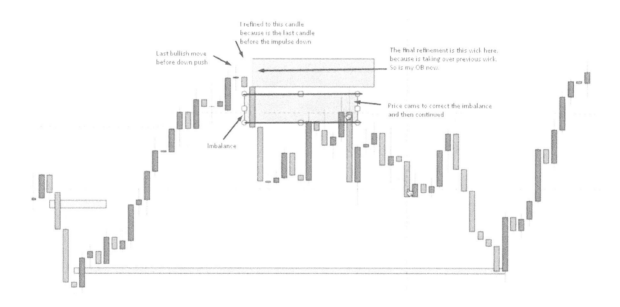

An imbalance is only truly something to think about when it has an OB next to it. For example, I can see that the price reached this low before the structure broke up here. This candle here represents the OB; I'll go into more detail about it by making reference to the next candle, which is also here. As you can see, this wick is an OB on its own because it is replacing the one that came before it.

I know there's an OB at that wick, either halfway through or at the base.

Where is the price change made? The base of this wick almost reacts and is attenuated; nonetheless, take note of where it reacts. Consequently, only sales are occurring, which corrects the imbalance.

After this candle, there is just pure selling since there are buyers inside that wick. The price has come and has subsequently moved in the proper direction to correct this imbalance.

It will strengthen my confidence that the OB is true and that the institutions were trading at that time, even though I won't use the imbalance for trading.

High and Lows

To start with this, we need to be able to recognize our highs and lows. We take it candle by candle to do this. So let's focus on the upcoming voyage.

Since we get our overall bias from the weekly, daily, and 4-hour periods, we will start with the weekly.

I decide to begin with weekly because it is quite high. Although we don't really change all that much every week, when we look at it this way, here is where our highs and lows are. We can see that even though the structures are breaking, our highs and lows won't change until this is done.

When the highs and lows are indicated, this is called a range, and it will be our trading range.

As a result, from this vantage point, price seems clearly negative, but it also seems bearish when viewed from the left. We don't need to worry about that just yet because pricing has just destroyed its fundamental support, which is why.

We just need to think about our next step in terms of the weekly bias till this range is broken, even if our bias is now negative.

New HH

When it comes to using the weekly to move our current highs and lows, we have lately surpassed the peak. Now, our high has been carried over into the next high. We may recognize our highs by using the wick that is highest for our high and the wick that is lowest for our low.

Now that the structure there was destroyed, the high point has been identified. We need to pinpoint the low's exact position. Thus, we want to identify which candle was broken if we descend and look at each one separately.

From this perspective, it will continue to create lows before producing highs, therefore this will now be the low.

Going ahead, that is our new low.

That is now our trading range.

bos

Now we bos the previous high
so now our bias has now gone
bullish

We have a bullish bias now that we have broken past the previous high, therefore we will be looking for buys inside this area.

It is also clear that we have the OB sitting here in terms of OBs, and that is basically where the price has responded, nearly approaching it.

Now that we've broken our high again, we'll transfer it to the most recent high and search for the previously set low.

We may so observe that we produced a low and a high simultaneously. Thus, at this moment, this candle broke the low of the previous one, creating a new low for us.

We may be hopeful about the price on a weekly basis, thus this is our weekly range. Put simply, the market's bullishness stems from the shattered bullish structure.

Our weekly highs and lows don't really shift all that often, so if we stop to think about it, we won't really be marking them out that much. These are significant actions.

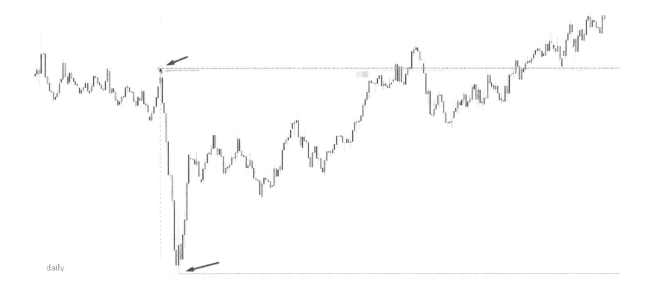

daily

Now that we have established our weekly high and low, if I restore the price back to its prior spot, we will proceed in the same manner every day. We shall thus ascertain our daily high and low.

We may now document our daily highs and lows as a result. Now, let's begin with this box.

It was therefore the time at which we experienced both our daily high and down. We don't need to go through our highs and lows till the structure has been demolished.

Since the building has been demolished, going forward, we shall refer to this as our peak and low points. The horizon marks the lowest point, and the highest point is visible   above   it.   That's   where   we   are   right   now.

The price is remains optimistic in this region as a result. This candle shattered the previously established low, which was from here, thus our low is now here, the lowest place.

Now that the low has been broken, we may move it to the candle low that was forming, where the high is still there.

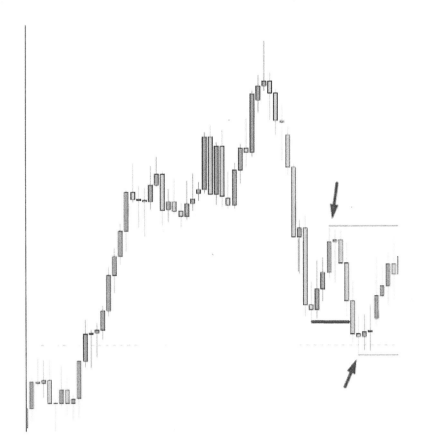

The building has crumbled again, so here is our low point, but the next peak will be higher than this one.
Now, we'll watch until one or both of these ranges are crossed.

The high has clearly been surpassed, but where is the low? The bottom is almost here. Below is our trading range, and the present price is bullish.

OB   refined
       OB

Now, by that, I mean that once we recognize that this is the OB, that it has been narrowed to this one, that we have a liquidity wick, and that the price has unquestionably rejected it and gone on, that's when we will start looking for buys. In fact, it responded here before continuing.

Here, where we set a new high, is where you'll find the bottom. As a result, this is the moment at which the candle's terms break.

this is not a bos

When it comes to bos, we like to have a candle body bos instead of only a wick. We shall use wicks to represent our lowest point when distinguishing our highs and lows, but for us, a wick is just a rejection. However, we won't proceed until both of them have been shattered because this is the highest produced that functioned as a low. Therefore, try not to worry when this happens.

Now that we have created a new high, we will relocate our old high to this one in order to find the low. Since this is the lowest point that has occurred, this will be the new range for our daily trading from this to this.

We created this high because we again upset the system here by this body, and now we're going to find the low, which is now.

As a result, the trading range has altered from this to this.

We have bos to the upside once again as we ascend to the highest position. When are we most vulnerable? To the best of our knowledge, this is our low..

Then, in a move that broke the low and is now our low, we had this downward move, but it was an odd one. Since that body destroyed the previous candle high, this one will now act as our high while we search for it.

Now that we can plainly see a high break, where is the low? The low is still good where it is.

Now that we've reached a peak and are once again breaking upward, we'll look for the lowest point. This is where the low will be, therefore that's where our trading range is currently.

And this will be our low point now that we have reached a new high, which is here.

We thus track our peaks and valleys in this way. We do the identical action on every single period.

Why do we do it, then?

We would want to know what range we are in. In an ideal world, we would want to retain information about the weekly high and low, even if I eliminated it. It was simply taken out for the video.

However, we shall record our weekly high and low for each time period. This candle represents both the high point and the low point for us this week.
We might additionally expand those lines with descriptions.

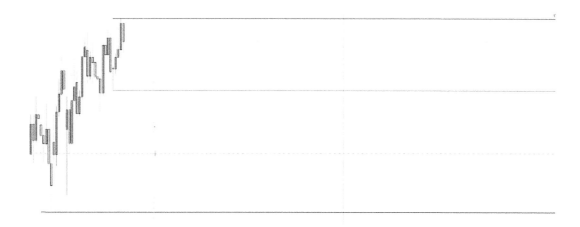

We will note our daily high and low points if we go to the daily. This means that the daily low, which is located here, and the daily high, which is located here, will somewhat overlap.
Once more, it fits the description of "daily high and low."

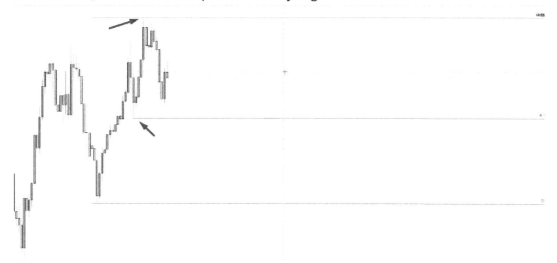

Let's now examine the H4 to determine the location of our high inside this range. The overlap is visible, and then we will do the H4 low and descend from the high, constantly keeping in mind to go backwards. Thus, this represents both our current low and the H4 low.

These are our trading ranges, so we can keep cutting the periods, which is why we are making highs and lows.
For example, we built our daily range on the upside of the previous daily move, which we capitalized on when we produced this H4 range.

Multiple timelines suggest that the pricing is optimistic. We now receive our buyers on a daily and weekly basis from H4.

On the H4, our trading range will be between this low and this high.

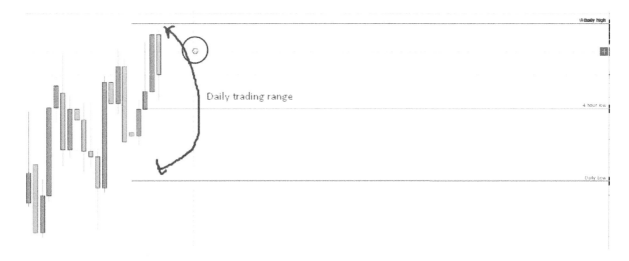

This low will be the starting point of the daily range, and it will rise to this high.

if price bos H4

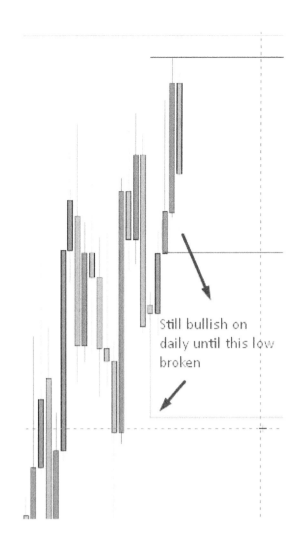

Still bullish on daily until this low broken

We will thus follow what the bias actually shows in order to stay inside the range we are tracking. For example, if price goes against the trend, the H4 chart will show bearish pricing, while the daily chart will show bullish pricing until this bottom is broken.

Made in the USA
Monee, IL
07 December 2024

72791240R00039